The

10-Minute Adult Activity Book

Dr Gareth Moore

Michael O'Mara Books Limited

First published in Great Britain in 2023 by
Michael O'Mara Books Limited
9 Lion Yard
Tremadoc Road
London SW4 7NQ

A CIP catalogue record for this book is available from the British Library.

Papers used by Michael O'Mara Books Limited are natural, recyclable products made from wood grown
in sustainable forests. The manufacturing processes conform to the environmental regulations of the
country of origin.

ISBN: 978-1-78929-504-7 in paperback print format

1 2 3 4 5 6 7 8 9 10

Designed and typeset by Gareth Moore

Featuring colouring pages by: Felicity French, Charlotte Pepper, Pimlada Phuapradit,
Pope Twins, Lizzie Preston, Angelika Scudamore

Printed and bound in Great Britain
by Bell and Bain Ltd, Glasgow

MIX
Paper from
responsible sources
FSC® C007785
FSC
www.fsc.org

Introduction

Take 10 minutes just for you with this book packed with over 130 puzzles and creative activities. Whether your idea of a break is to solve a sudoku or simply to peacefully colour in a picture, this book has you covered. Or if you'd prefer to try a word puzzle, then give the word searches and crosswords a go.

Clear your mind of the day's distractions and settle down to the task at hand. Once you have your pens and pencils in front of you, you're ready to go – everything else you'll need can be found within the bounds of this book. Some days, when you have more time, you might feel like attempting a colouring page; while on others you might fancy more of a challenge, which is why on the puzzle pages I've put a 'stopwatch' graphic at the top – how long did each puzzle take you? Can you complete them within 10 minutes?

You could start your mindfulness session with one of the Spot the differences, dot-to-dots or mazes – these puzzles will require just enough focus that you are paying attention to the task, but not so much that they'll feel like work!

Or, if you fancy a real challenge, then try the bumper-size hanjie puzzles. These reveal hidden pictures as you solve them, based on the clues around the grid. See below for full instructions.

The puzzles are not arranged in any particular order, except that the later 'Spot the differences' have more changes to find, and the later hanjie puzzles are even bigger than the rest. Where needed, solutions are given at the back of the book.

So jump in and have fun. The 'stopwatch' is there for you to note your timings and chart your progress should you wish to do so.

Enjoy the puzzles!

Fences instructions
Draw horizontal and vertical lines to form a single loop that visits every dot in turn, without revisiting a dot or crossing over itself.

Hanjie instructions
Shade some squares according to the given clue numbers. The clues provide, in reading order from left to right or top to bottom, the length of every run of consecutive shaded squares in each row and column. There must be a gap of at least one empty square between each run of shaded squares in the same row or column.

Sudoku instructions
Place a digit from 1 to 9 into each empty square, so no digit repeats in any row, column or bold-lined 3×3 box.

Solution on
page 113

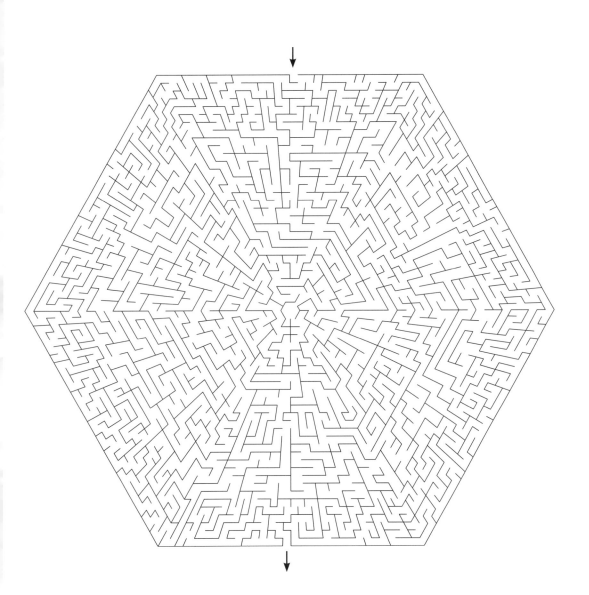

3: Spot the difference

There are 10 differences to find.

Solution on page 113

Join dots in increasing numerical order, starting each path at a star. Lift your pen each time you reach a hollow star.

Solution on
page 113

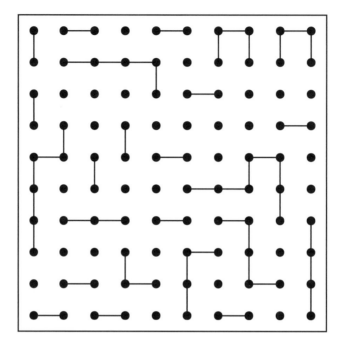

Solution on
page 113

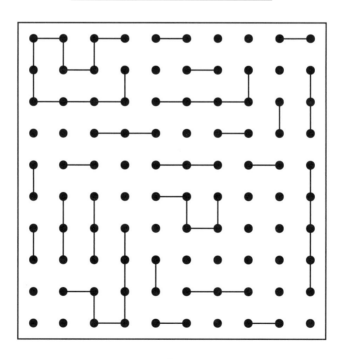

8: Crossword

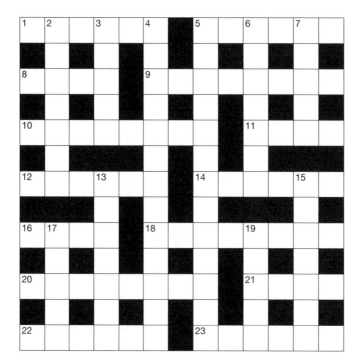

Across
1 Soak up (6)
5 Evacuates from a pilot's seat (6)
8 Long-handled gardening tools (4)
9 Incidentally (2,3,3)
10 Bleach (8)
11 Coat with gold (4)
12 Arts journalist, perhaps (6)
14 Helping (6)
16 Emotion when in danger (4)
18 Lines of descent (8)
20 Battle (8)
21 Plant with large, showy flowers (4)
22 Ball (6)
23 However (6)

Down
2 Male sibling (7)
3 Start (5)
4 The Black Death (7,6)
5 Amusement (13)
6 Appeared (7)
7 Track (5)
13 Torment (7)
15 Requiring (7)
17 Finish a meal (3,2)
19 Compadre (5)

9: It means 'hello'

```
O K R I I A S E B N I J I N I
O J A E A R A T O K Z N L N A
A A A R O H L I J O D J O L E
I X H M B T A E A N R N U O T
U U O C B N A V B N A B O O S
A E L H N O M A A I V N A U A
Z O A J D I A R H C O I H U M
I L O A A B X D R H C A I N A
O H A N A O O Z A I O V N I N
A S A U K N E M M W O K A A A
A O U V L J R O A A R I O B A
R O N H U O H U R A J O U N U
A E N J W U A S V E I K I I L
J B A B U R H O I H I Z C A E
D O S A L V E A V A H E S S H
```

AHOJ
BONJOUR
BULA
CIAO
HALO
HOLA
JAMBO
KONNICHIWA
MARHABA
NAMASTE
NI HAO
SAIN BAINUU
SALAAM
SALVE
SANNU
SVEIKI
SZIA
XIN CHAO
ZDRAVEITE
ZDRAVO

10: Spot the difference

There are 10 differences to find.

Picture clue: Celebratory cake

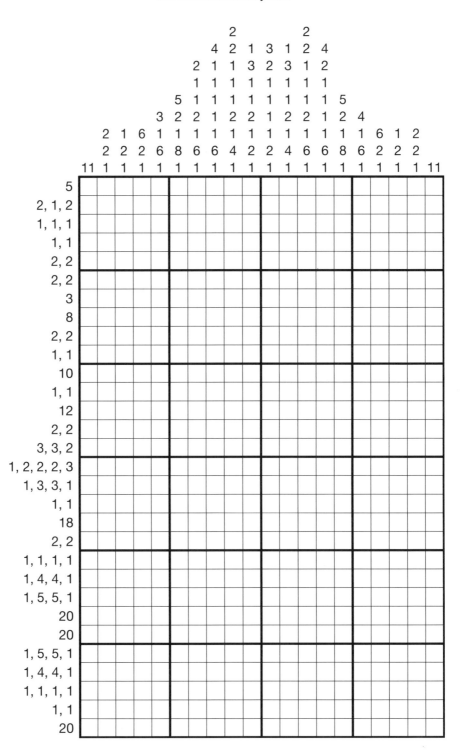

13: Spot the difference

Solution on page 114

There are 10 differences to find.

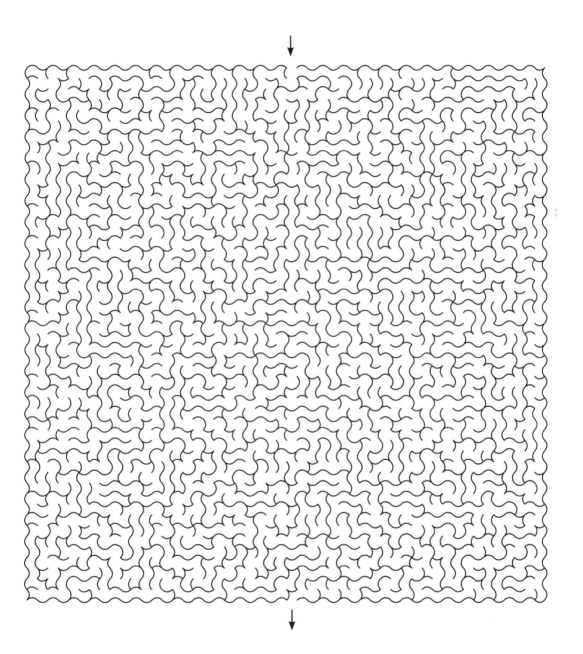

Join dots in increasing numerical order, starting each path at a star. Lift your pen each time you reach a hollow star.

17: Crossword

Solution on page 115

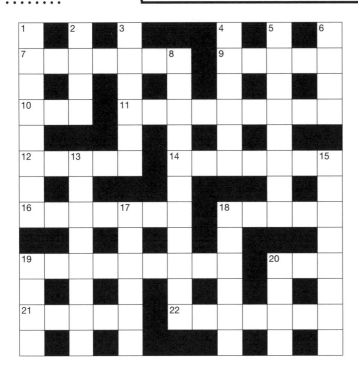

Across

7 Famous conductors (7)
9 Braid (5)
10 Hit a ball over an opponent (3)
11 A set of foundation stories (9)
12 Vulgar (5)
14 Silhouette (7)
16 Vivid pictorial impression (7)
18 Preserve (3,2)
19 Elucidates (9)
20 Existed (3)
21 At that position (5)
22 Higher in value (7)

Down

1 Tacit (8)
2 Parsley or sage (4)
3 Hinder progress (6)
4 Most extreme (6)
5 Speed (8)
6 Kids' spotting game (1,3)
8 Establishing (11)
13 Impartial (8)
15 Revelation (8)
17 Amended (6)
18 Included on a register (6)
19 Reductions in service (4)
20 Jokers (4)

18: Yoga Mudras

Solution on page 115

A	P	K	I	V	A	D	B	R	A	I	R	S	J	A
K	P	N	A	Y	A	D	I	R	H	H	H	M	P	U
A	U	H	A	Y	U	S	I	V	V	A	H	A	I	N
S	N	D	N	Y	H	P	K	A	K	N	N	N	K	H
H	M	A	A	A	H	M	R	I	I	A	A	N	T	S
I	A	V	K	A	A	I	N	A	S	Y	A	N	V	I
A	N	T	D	N	A	I	A	A	A	I	I	N	N	V
H	I	A	D	H	S	N	A	T	A	D	A	G	I	H
A	I	U	B	A	D	A	S	A	Y	A	U	I	U	V
U	K	K	K	N	I	I	T	Y	A	N	U	K	K	I
I	V	H	A	I	B	M	I	N	N	U	Y	R	I	G
H	I	R	L	K	A	V	I	U	A	R	A	O	Y	N
I	P	R	I	T	H	V	I	H	Y	A	R	A	N	N
A	N	A	R	P	I	N	S	S	H	V	N	A	I	I
M	V	I	A	N	J	A	L	I	D	A	A	T	N	H

AKASHI
ANJALI
APANA
BHAIRAV
DHYANA
GYANA
HAKINI
HRIDAYA
KAKI
MANDUKI
PRANA
PRITHVI
SHAKTI
SHUNYA
TADAGI
UNMANI
VARUNA
VAYU
VISHNU
YONI

19: Spot the difference

Solution on
page 115

There are 10 differences to find.

Solution on
page 115

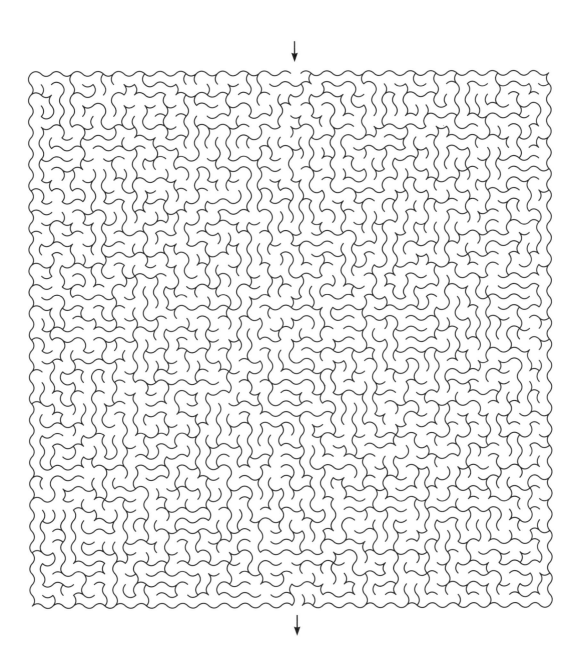

Solution on
page 115

Join dots in increasing numerical order, starting each path at a star. Lift your pen each time you reach a hollow star.

23

25: Square Maze

Solution on page 115

27: Dot to Dot

Join dots in increasing numerical order, starting each path at a star. Lift your pen each time you reach a hollow star.

28: Angular Maze

Solution on page 116

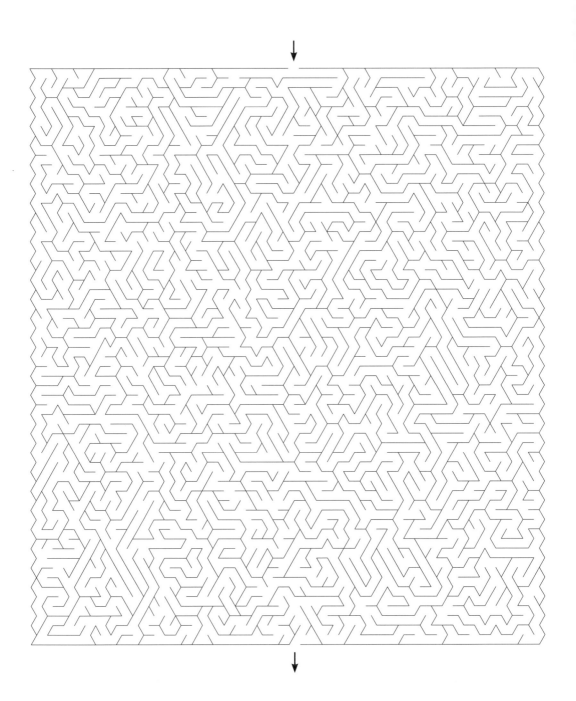

30: Fences

Solution on page 116

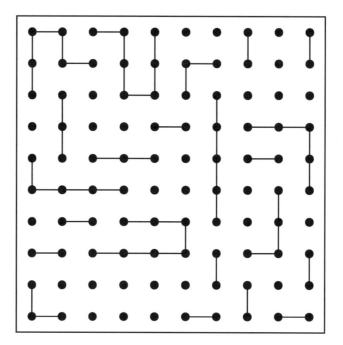

31: Fences

Solution on page 116

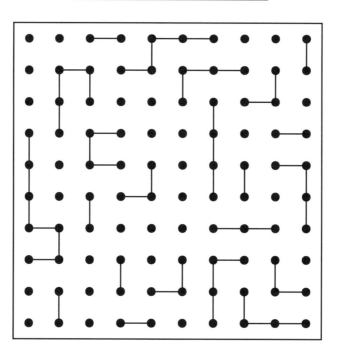

Solution on page 116

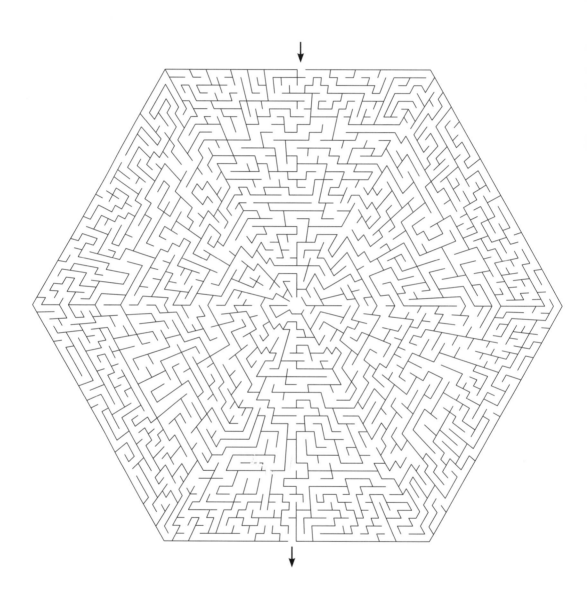

34: Spot the difference

There are 10 differences to find.

Solution on page 117

Picture clue: Night-time watcher

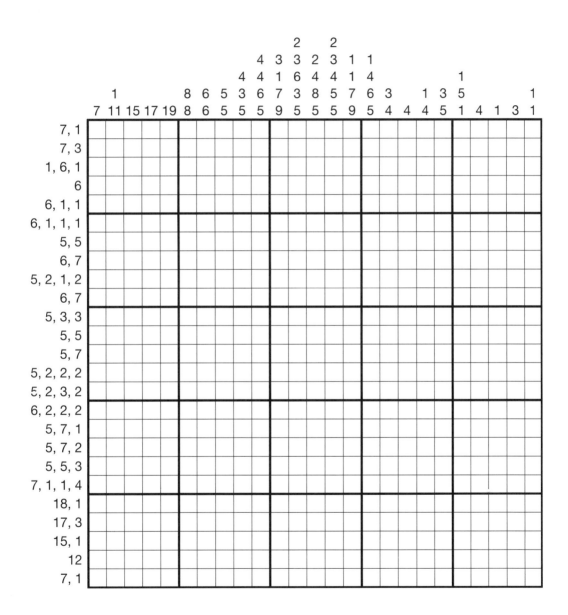

37: Crossword

Solution on page 117

Across
1 Long, tapering, edible root (7)
5 Soft, sheepskin leather (5)
9 Form an idea of (13)
10 Eastern (8)
11 Extremely serious or urgent (4)
12 Spying (9)
16 Whisker (4)
17 Disclosed (8)
19 Communicating in writing (13)
21 Jewish teacher (5)
22 Mischievous (7)

Down
2 On a ship or plane (6)
3 Heir (9)
4 Information submitted to a computer (5)
6 Lubricate (3)
7 Possible danger (6)
8 Thin cotton cloth (6)
11 Ruthless (3-3-3)
13 Sudden arrival (6)
14 Triangular Indian snack (6)
15 Snack legume, often roasted or salted (6)
18 Orchestral stringed instrument (5)
20 Umbrella spoke (3)

38: Gods of the World

Solution on page 117

```
M D H I I S I S R E T I P U J
U A L T P P S A R A S W A T I
I R U G N O D I E S O P E B I
O U L S I B U N A Y I L R B S
H M R U P N E I R K U T S E D
R A H Y N S I U A C E I N U G
O I A E U S C L P R G I R S U
H R I I R R I R S A D G U I U
T N G U E M K R N O A E T H D
E A E M S C E A I S Z A I A P
E B M P O D Z S S S V R I I E
O U I G T I A A S R O K S N N
A I O A R U K W A O O R I U U
R S N R K O N P I K O N M A U
A O L L O P A E U I I E E S I
```

ANUBIS
APOLLO
DAIKOKU
DARUMA
DURGA
HERMES
ISIS
IZANAGI
JUPITER
KALI
MERCURY
NABU
NEPTUNE
ODIN
OSIRIS
PARVATI
POSEIDON
SARASWATI
THOR
ZEUS

Join dots in increasing numerical order, starting each path at a star. Lift your pen each time you reach a hollow star.

		2	9			5	1	
		9		3		2		
7	6						4	9
5				2				4
	3		8		4		5	
9				7				8
4	9						2	1
		7		8		4		
		5	1			9	3	

4		5				6		3
		1				7		
3	2			7			5	1
			8	2	5			
		3	6		4	5		
			7	9	3			
1	8			4			6	5
		9				1		
6		7				8		4

Solution on
page 118

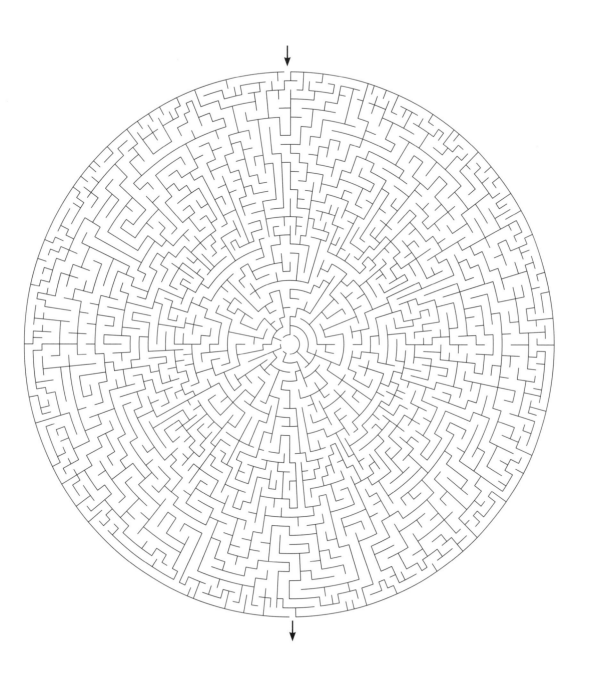

46: Crossword

Solution on page 118

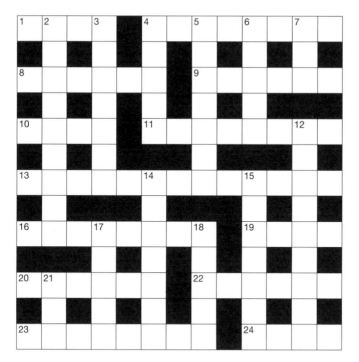

Across
1 Appear (4)
4 Parts (8)
8 Primarily (6)
9 Sounds (6)
10 Aquatic vertebrate (4)
11 Least old (8)
13 Laid-back popular music (4,9)
16 Word for word (8)
19 Shower (4)
20 Jumped suddenly (6)
22 Stringed instrument (6)
23 Of momentous importance (8)
24 Joy; delight (4)

Down
2 Put an end to (9)
3 Twelve times a year (7)
4 In a deceitful way (5)
5 Confer (7)
6 Covering with frozen water (5)
7 Birth name (3)
12 Consortium (9)
14 Whole number (7)
15 Caring for (7)
17 Explosion (5)
18 Conjuring (5)
21 Penultimate Greek letter (3)

47: Types of Table

Solution on page 118

```
N T B P G A R D E N S R N G D
G C A S I N N E T E L B A T G
N C B E N C H A I N G C P N I
I O S T E N G S E N I O I R N
N F N F N A F S I R B T E P D
I F H F T O T W E I F S I G F
D E G E L I A K L A R C F N E
F E L D N R O L R E N S D I G
G E I G D P I D N I D N R T T
G N C T G A G E C R E D T I R
G S D A R R G N B H S N C R E
S E R D T I I D E T K A C W S
I E D E G G E L E E R H T T T
D D D R E S S I N G N E I D L
E R G G G A G N I W E S N S E
```

BENCH
BILLIARD
COFFEE
DESK
DINING
DRAFTING
DRAWING
DRESSING
FOLDING
GARDEN
GATELEG
NESTING
PICNIC
POKER
SEWING
SIDE
TABLE-TENNIS
THREE-LEGGED
TRESTLE
WRITING

Solution on
page 118

Join dots in increasing numerical order, starting each path at a star. Lift your pen each time you reach a hollow star.

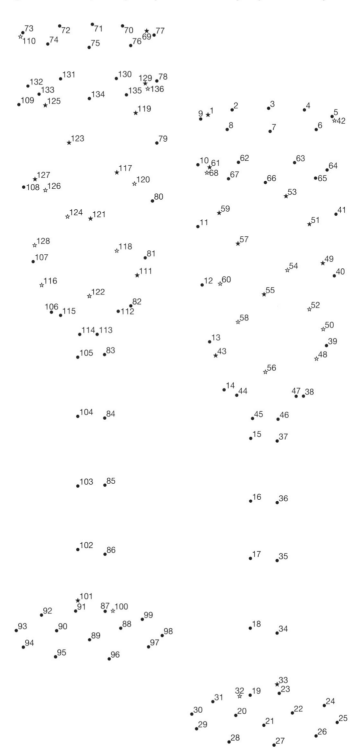

Solution on
page 118

Join dots in increasing numerical order, starting each path at a star. Lift your pen each time you reach a hollow star.

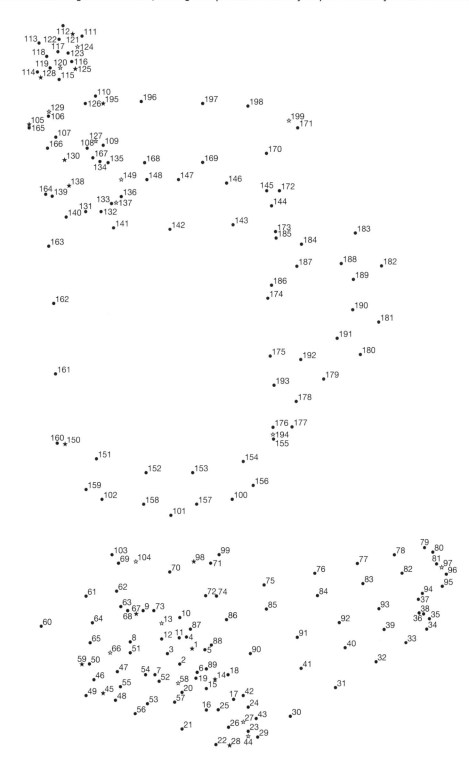

53: Crossword

Solution on page 118

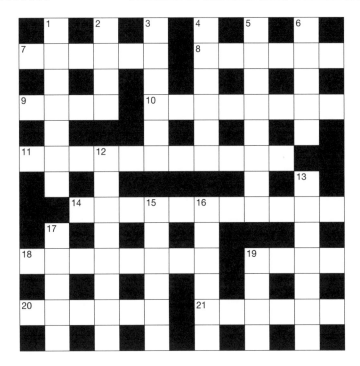

Across

7 Diversion (6)
8 Split into stages (6)
9 'Right away!', in hospital (4)
10 Extreme force (8)
11 Fortune-telling globe (7,4)
14 Of Antarctica or of Africa, eg (11)
18 Sobriquet (8)
19 Crowds of troublemakers (4)
20 Word formed from a person's name (6)
21 Naval standard (6)

Down

1 Go from the beginning again (7)
2 Type (4)
3 Mostly useless information (6)
4 Self-assurance (6)
5 Advance strategy (4,4)
6 Long, hard seat (5)
12 Shameful (8)
13 Trash (7)
15 Wound (6)
16 Obligatory (6)
17 Like cloud fragments (5)
19 Be absorbed in thought (4)

54: Types of Silk

Solution on page 119

H	T	E	S	A	N	D	A	L	O	I	E	S	O	A
C	O	R	N	C	S	E	L	E	T	L	A	U	N	P
N	R	R	R	S	E	R	I	C	V	S	V	R	Y	F
G	N	E	X	R	T	T	O	N	P	A	G	A	I	U
M	P	N	L	O	O	T	B	L	U	B	E	H	I	T
E	N	N	L	T	L	R	P	M	L	O	T	L	C	A
U	F	O	U	C	O	F	A	N	E	C	A	N	S	U
E	A	L	N	C	S	R	E	D	M	N	B	A	R	V
P	L	R	A	I	T	G	A	O	B	I	B	N	O	A
E	N	D	A	L	N	I	S	T	P	K	Y	I	V	O
R	E	T	E	V	L	E	V	O	L	S	L	T	A	T
A	A	A	V	U	R	A	Z	A	G	A	N	A	N	A
C	U	I	N	O	I	P	U	D	S	A	S	S	O	S
R	E	E	B	S	A	I	U	L	U	P	S	R	E	A
R	N	A	T	H	C	L	O	E	V	B	E	C	D	R

ATLAS
BROCADE
CORN
CREPE
DUPION
FLOX
GAZAR
KINCOB
NINON
PULU
SANDAL
SATIN
SERIC
SLEAVE
SURAH
TABBY
TASAR
TRAM
TULLE
VELVET

55: Hanjie

Picture clue: Made it to the top

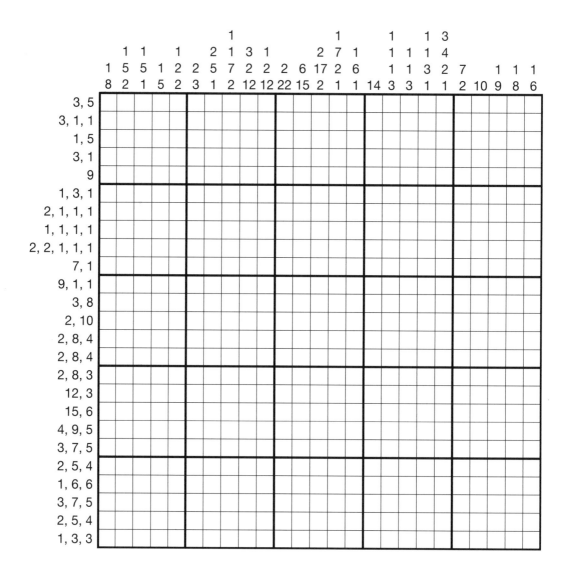

Solution on
page 119

Join dots in increasing numerical order, starting each path at a star. Lift your pen each time you reach a hollow star.

There are 10 differences to find.

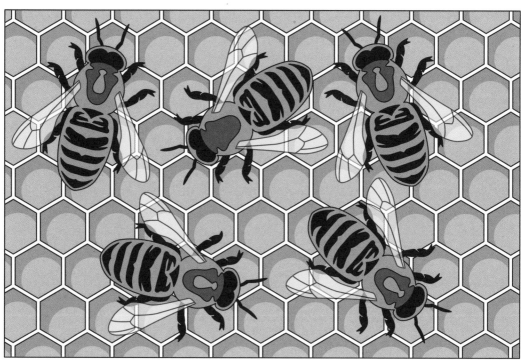

Join dots in increasing numerical order, starting each path at a star. Lift your pen each time you reach a hollow star.

60: Spot the difference

Solution on page 119

There are 15 differences to find.

Solution on page 120

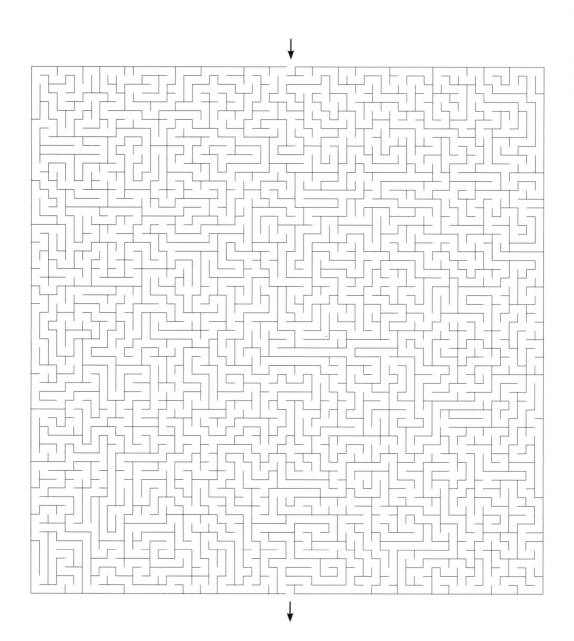

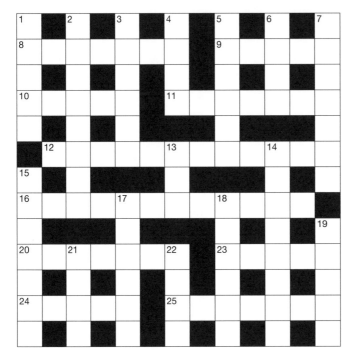

Across
8 Gather (7)
9 Allude (5)
10 Miley Cyrus move (5)
11 Disparage (5,2)
12 Impediments (12)
16 Insouciance (12)
20 Develop in a promising way (5,2)
23 Main bodily artery (5)
24 Lawful (5)
25 Sways back and forth (7)

Down
1 Malice (5)
2 Clergyman (8)
3 You might carry water in it (6)
4 Collections (4)
5 Take into custody (6)
6 Way off (4)
7 Objection (7)
13 Frozen water (3)
14 Took place (8)
15 Initially (7)
17 Lacking strength (6)
18 Pencil remover (6)
19 Decision-making power (3-2)
21 Pond organism (4)
22 Lays (4)

64: Dog Training

Solution on
page 120

P	C	E	E	L	T	S	I	H	W	W	H	C	L	T
D	P	M	U	J	E	N	O	P	F	W	O	C	E	W
S	T	E	L	E	A	O	C	O	T	L	N	H	I	L
E	E	E	L	T	N	C	O	U	L	I	A	I	S	D
L	E	N	E	P	L	D	N	A	R	R	E	F	Y	R
H	L	E	U	I	L	N	R	O	N	C	R	O	A	A
I	I	P	C	I	E	O	K	E	N	P	T	T	L	W
U	P	K	A	L	R	L	S	E	O	P	S	C	E	E
Y	E	D	U	E	A	S	I	F	I	O	I	Y	W	R
R	P	L	C	W	S	D	H	E	N	I	L	L	A	B
C	K	A	L	T	E	H	E	T	I	Y	R	S	S	E
C	L	T	A	B	I	L	R	C	S	S	N	I	E	L
L	S	E	O	L	C	T	H	H	K	T	R	R	E	L
H	R	R	E	S	I	A	R	P	A	F	I	B	S	A
T	A	C	W	R	J	Y	T	I	L	I	G	A	I	L

AGILITY
BALL
CLICKER
COLLAR
FETCH
FOOD
HARNESS
HEEL
JUMP
OBEDIENCE
PRAISE
PUPPY
RECALL
REWARD
SEE-SAW
TOY
TREATS
TUNNEL
WALK
WHISTLE

65: Dot to Dot

Join dots in increasing numerical order, starting each path at a star. Lift your pen each time you reach a hollow star.

			2		3			
		2		8		4		
	7		6		9		8	
1		4				3		2
	9						5	
7		5				8		4
	2		9		8		1	
		3		2		6		
			3		4			

	9	1				2	3	
4			3		2			6
2								7
	1		9		6		5	
				5				
	5		4		1		2	
6								5
1			7		5			2
	4	8				7	1	

69: Dot to Dot

Solution on
page 121

Join dots in increasing numerical order, starting each path at a star. Lift your pen each time you reach a hollow star.

Solution on page 121

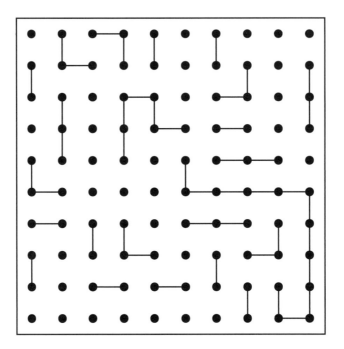

....

72: Fences

Solution on page 121

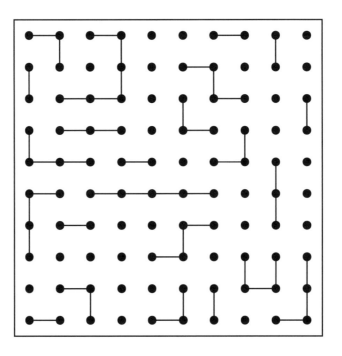

73: Dot to Dot

Join dots in increasing numerical order, starting each path at a star. Lift your pen each time you reach a hollow star.

75: Crossword

Solution on page 121

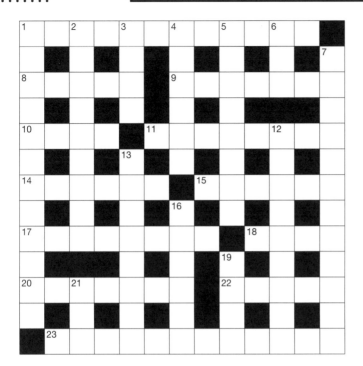

Across
1 Heat measurements (12)
8 Concur (5)
9 Popular poison, in literature (7)
10 Hitch (4)
11 Indian consort (8)
14 Kind of (2,1,3)
15 Threefold (6)
17 Plot outline (8)
18 Angle (4)
20 Acquires (7)
22 Before (5)
23 Concerned only with the present (4,3,2,3)

Down
1 Broadcast (12)
2 Citrus fruit preserve (9)
3 Pitcher (4)
4 Online user's self-image (6)
5 On a higher floor (8)
6 A period of several eras (3)
7 Without deliberate intent (12)
12 Designated (9)
13 Model; prototype (8)
16 Religious festival (6)
19 Fine, dry powder (4)
21 Hilltop (3)

76: Food-product oils

Solution on page 121

P	E	C	A	N	E	W	A	L	N	U	T	L	B	O
D	U	P	E	U	R	H	D	A	A	I	O	P	E	T
E	L	U	T	U	N	E	N	I	P	I	E	N	E	U
L	C	E	D	C	D	A	W	M	L	A	P	N	C	I
S	O	E	M	E	A	U	Y	O	N	S	A	E	H	E
E	U	L	A	O	E	A	I	U	L	E	O	L	N	R
S	W	I	C	S	N	S	T	E	B	F	P	E	U	D
A	E	N	A	P	C	H	E	Y	N	I	N	E	T	N
M	H	S	D	N	P	U	O	P	S	T	E	U	I	O
E	S	E	A	U	E	S	E	T	A	N	I	A	S	M
E	A	E	M	L	N	U	A	O	C	R	U	A	C	L
V	C	D	I	T	A	C	O	C	O	N	U	T	C	A
I	L	O	A	L	H	N	C	A	N	S	C	N	N	A
L	B	L	P	I	H	A	Z	E	L	N	U	T	R	L
O	A	E	O	E	U	N	E	A	I	E	P	O	S	S

ACAI
ALMOND
BEECHNUT
CASHEW
COCONUT
HAZELNUT
LEMON
LINSEED
MACADAMIA
OLIVE
PALM
PEANUT
PECAN
PINE NUT
PISTACHIO
RAPESEED
SESAME
SOYBEAN
SUNFLOWER
WALNUT

77: Hanjie

Solution on
page 122

Picture clue: Looks comfy

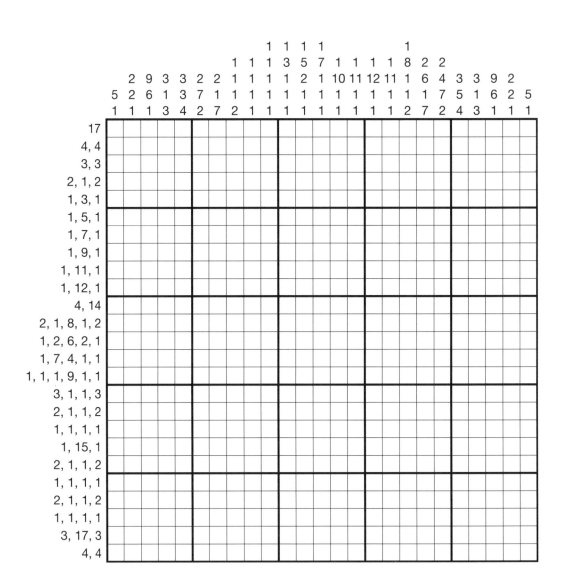

Solution on
page 122

Join dots in increasing numerical order, starting each path at a star. Lift your pen each time you reach a hollow star.

Solution on page 122

4			3		7			1
	3			5			4	
			1	9	4			
9		8				5		7
	2	5				6	1	
3		6				8		4
			4	6	8			
	8			2			3	
5			9		1			2

Solution on page 122

	2		6		9		7	
1				8				5
		4		3		8		
5				7				6
	4	7	8		2	3	1	
3				4				7
		1		6		7		
2				9				4
	3		4		7		5	

Solution on
page 122

Join dots in increasing numerical order, starting each path at a star. Lift your pen each time you reach a hollow star.

84: Musical techniques

```
A P O R T A M E N T O E S O I
S F O R Z A N D O O C C I N O
O V R P I Z Z I C A T O T E I
N T A P P O G G I A T U R A P
I N A S A O N I D R O S N O C
D A A L A O A R P E G G I O G
R P R L L R C I T T U T U T L
O S U U S E U O P O B A S A I
S P A N T T T L O T I O R S
A I T O A A A R A L R I D B S
Z C R T G C D C A R E T A I A
N C U E Z A O R C M O G A V N
E A L T R S L R O A O L N T D
S T M T O R A E D C T C O O O
O O M I S S I T L A S O O C N
```

ALTISSIMO
APPOGGIATURA
ARPEGGIO
COL LEGNO
COLORATURA
CON SORDINO
GLISSANDO
LEGATO
MARTELLATO
PIZZICATO
PORTAMENTO
PORTATO
SCORDATURA
SENZA SORDINO
SFORZANDO
SPICCATO
STACCATO
TUTTI
UNA CORDA
VIBRATO

85: Cruise holiday

Solution on page 123

```
E O N O T O I U P R D I S B T
E E E O C T T E N D E R I P A
O R G E I I T S I N A I P N A
G C U A S S S I O B U F F E T
I A E T G T R A D C C A B I N
L Q D A C G E U T U S D A B O
L D U E N E U W C C I I C C T
Y N C I C K L L A X A B D L G
N R S E Z K S R U R E A O E R
O I C A P T A I N N D I C U Y
C U A C I E N K A R A O K E T
L S R P P P I L A Q L O O P R
A C R O O M S E R V I C E O O
B T C K F A E C G B A V T I P
E N C N S H I P S S T C P A P
```

BALCONY
BUFFET
CABIN
CAPTAIN
DECK
DISCO
EXCURSION
KARAOKE
LECTURE
LUGGAGE
OCEAN
PIANIST
POOL
PORT
QUIZ
ROOM SERVICE
SHIP
SPA
STEWARD
TENDER

86: Dot to Dot

Join dots in increasing numerical order, starting each path at a star. Lift your pen each time you reach a hollow star.

Solution on
page 123

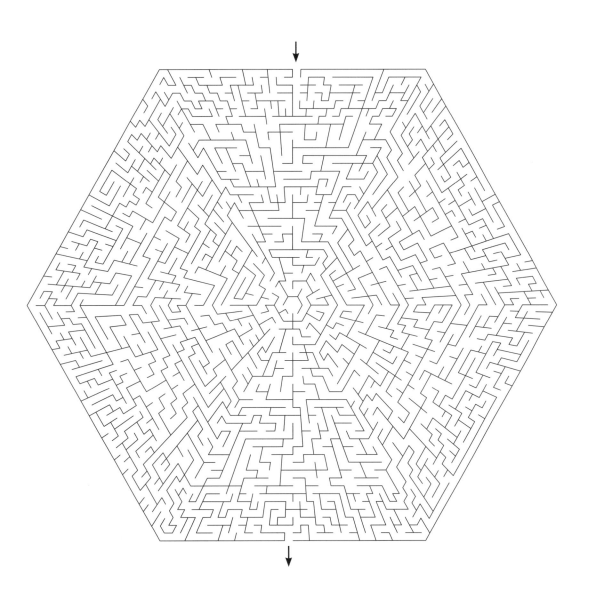

Solution on
page 123

Join dots in increasing numerical order, starting each path at a star. Lift your pen each time you reach a hollow star.

91: Spot the difference

Solution on
page 123

There are 15 differences to find.

Join dots in increasing numerical order, starting each path at a star. Lift your pen each time you reach a hollow star.

94: Fences

Solution on
page 124

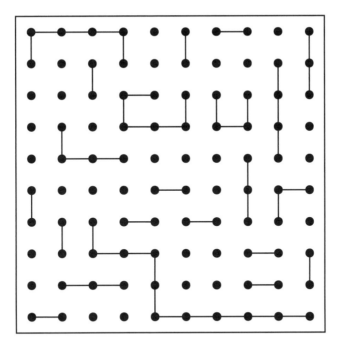

95: Fences

Solution on
page 124

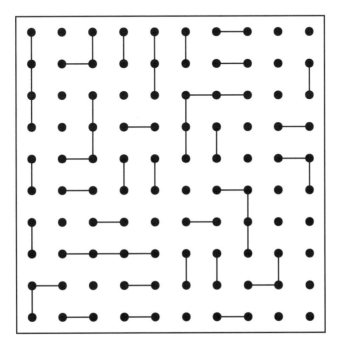

Join dots in increasing numerical order, starting each path at a star. Lift your pen each time you reach a hollow star.

98: Crossword

Solution on page 124

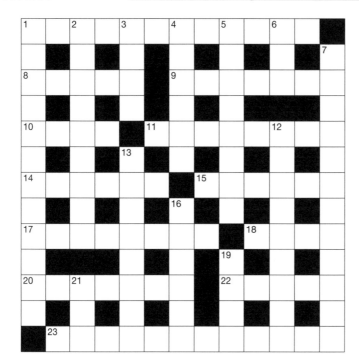

Across
1 Not persuasive (12)
8 Distinct period (5)
9 Small discussion group (7)
10 Gemstone (4)
11 Sencha or Longjing (5,3)
14 False (6)
15 Feel remorse for (6)
17 Portend (8)
18 Den (4)
20 Seeing (7)
22 Goodbye (5)
23 'Drink up!' (4,3,5)

Down
1 Fruitless (12)
2 Temperament (9)
3 Repeated refusals (4)
4 Put in (6)
5 Vies (8)
6 Religious woman (3)
7 Major advance (12)
12 Physical treatment expert (9)
13 Span (8)
16 Extent (6)
19 Container for washing in (4)
21 Self-image (3)

99: Currencies

Solution on page 124

N	U	O	A	D	W	E	L	D	A	R	Y	F	L	E
K	O	N	A	I	P	O	D	A	N	U	L	D	D	L
T	R	B	D	E	A	O	D	O	E	U	E	Y	K	A
A	B	O	S	F	L	O	R	I	N	R	O	R	Y	K
L	P	O	N	A	H	U	N	D	N	E	E	P	A	Z
E	W	C	B	E	A	N	Y	O	D	U	U	A	T	N
U	O	N	R	B	A	H	T	N	N	L	R	L	K	L
O	N	A	N	D	R	A	O	R	A	O	O	R	U	N
R	E	R	A	K	I	R	L	A	U	A	T	U	N	N
T	N	F	A	A	E	N	Z	R	Y	P	N	N	A	N
R	D	N	M	R	P	D	A	L	U	K	E	T	E	F
D	R	A	N	D	R	R	R	R	I	A	A	E	W	Y
P	A	A	H	O	L	B	L	A	U	N	R	A	A	P
E	N	N	N	N	K	M	O	Y	M	N	I	A	U	O
P	E	N	T	R	I	U	A	N	O	O	L	A	I	U

BAHT
DINAR
DRAM
EURO
FLORIN
FRANC
KRONE
KUNA
KYAT
LEU
LIRA
PESO
POUND
RAND
REAL
RUPEE
WON
YEN
YUAN
ZLOTY

101: Hanjie

Solution on
page 124

Picture clue: Work it out

Column clues (top):

```
                              1
                              3              1              1
                              1        1  5              5
                        1  1        1  1           1
                  1           1  1        1  1           1           1
            1  5  1     1  1  1  1  1  1        1  1        1  1
            1  1  1     1  1  1  1  1  1  1     1  1  1     1  1
            2  2  2     1  1  3  1  3  1  1     1  1  1     1  3  1
            2  2  2  1  3  1  3  1  3  1  3     3  1  3  1  1  1  1
            2  2  2  1  3  1  3  1  3  1  3  1  3  1  3  3  3  3  3
         2  2  2  2  3  3  1  1  1  1  1  3  3  3  1  3  1  3  3  3  2
      11 2  2  2  2  1  3  1  1  1  1  1  3  1  3  1  3  1  7  7  7  2 11
      17 3  1  1  1  1  1  1  1  1  1  1  1  1  1  1  1  1  1  1  1  3 17
```

Row clues (left):

21	
2, 2	
1, 1	
1, 1, 3, 3, 1, 1, 3, 1	
1, 1, 1, 1, 1, 1, 1, 1	
1, 1, 3, 3, 3, 3, 1	
1, 1, 1, 1, 1, 1, 1, 1	
1, 1, 3, 3, 1, 3, 1	
1, 1	
2, 2	
23	
2, 2	
1, 1	
1, 3, 3, 3, 3, 3, 1	
1, 3, 1, 1, 1, 1, 1, 1, 3, 1	
1, 3, 3, 3, 3, 1	
1, 3, 1	
1, 3, 3, 3, 3, 3, 1	
1, 1, 1, 1, 1, 1, 1, 3, 1	
1, 3, 3, 3, 3, 3, 1	
1, 3, 1	
1, 3, 3, 3, 3, 1	
1, 3, 1, 1, 1, 1, 1, 3, 1	
1, 3, 3, 3, 3, 3, 1	
1, 3, 1	
1, 3, 7, 3, 3, 1	
1, 3, 1, 1, 1, 1, 3, 1	
2, 7, 3, 3, 2	
1, 1	
23	

102: Spot the difference

There are 15 differences to find.

Solution on
page 125

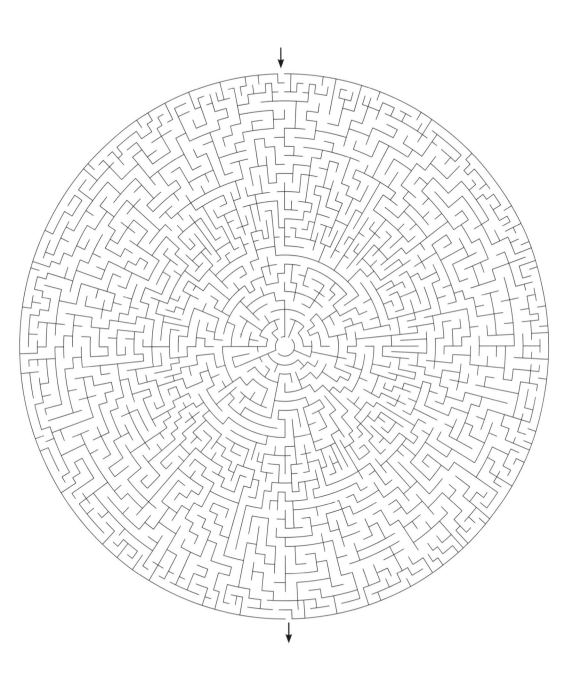

106: Dot to Dot

Join dots in increasing numerical order, starting each path at a star. Lift your pen each time you reach a hollow star.

Picture clue: Tropical taste

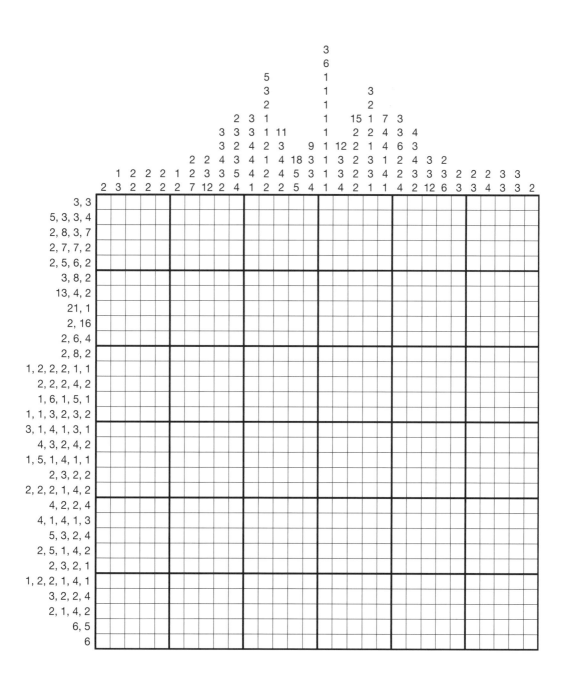

109: Circular Maze

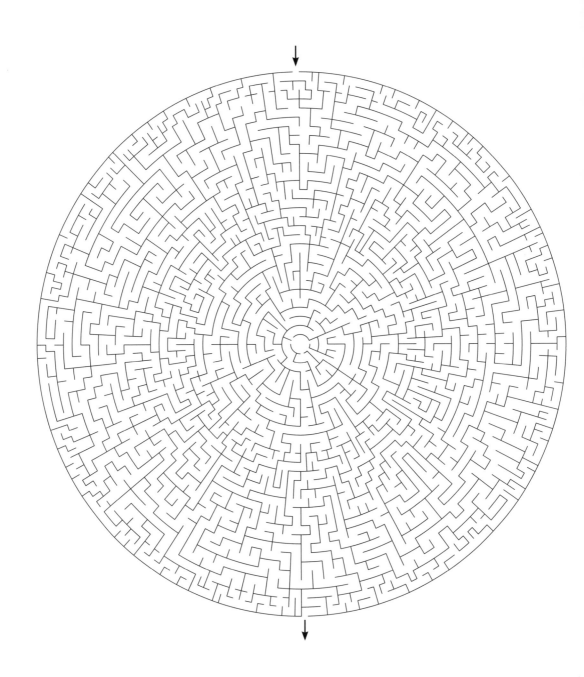

110: Spot the difference

Solution on
page 125

There are 15 differences to find.

111: Crossword

Solution on page 126

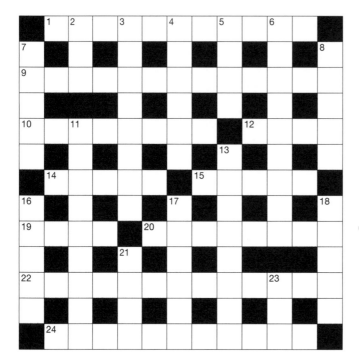

Across
1 Dislike of everyone (11)
9 In chaotic haste (6-7)
10 Formal teaching sessions (8)
12 Police (4)
14 Typefaces (5)
15 What Britain is a land of, according to Elgar (5)
19 Afresh; another time (4)
20 Certain (8)
22 Protecting spirit (8,5)
24 Famous individual (11)

Down
2 Unwell (3)
3 Okay (8)
4 Sampled (6)
5 Was sorry for (4)
6 Dried petal mix (9)
7 Ledge (5)
8 Precipitous market drop (5)
11 Collaborate (9)
13 On the whole (3,2,3)
16 React to a joke, perhaps (5)
17 Continue (6)
18 Lunch and dinner, eg (5)
21 Appends (4)
23 Understood (3)

112: Homophone words

Solution on page 126

```
U M R W O E D E R E A N A I E
F E R D E E L B W R E Z I A M
W A A E L M R O R I A D I W E
L I I W X B W L L Y E S S D M
Y W O W W D E S S A P L E H A
N B I O A E O A S O E A M E I
X E B W E M I A L I R S W E N
W F O R A O B G G E A B G L L
E R L L L N W W H L R A B W O
I N O L B E M E L E I A R A A
P A F A P A L O W T D A U L L
N I R L O B W E O X A R I F X
B S U R P E D W A N O H S A L
B M E I D A O H O U R E E A W
B R R N O X E W E Y R S U O W
```

ALLOWED
BOAR
BOWLED
BREWED
BRUISE
DEAR
FLAW
GAIT
HEEL
HOUR
LOAN
LYNX
MAIN
MAIZE
PASSED
PLUMB
ROAM
ROW
WEIGHED
YEW

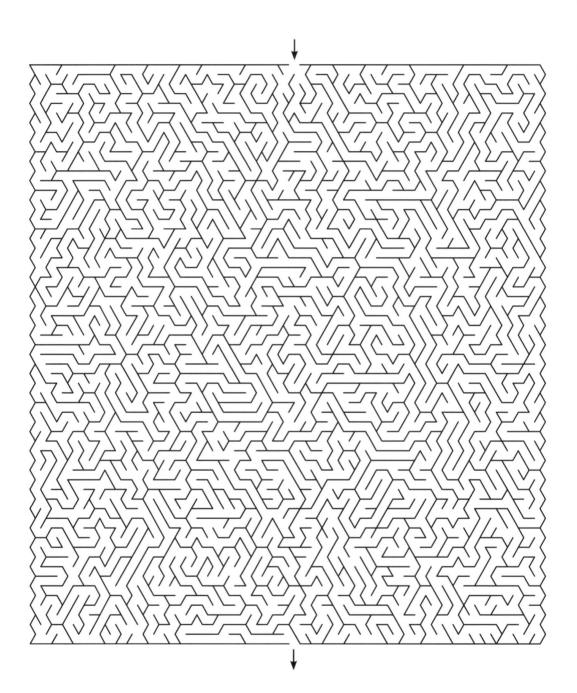

Solution on
page 126

Join dots in increasing numerical order, starting each path at a star. Lift your pen each time you reach a hollow star.

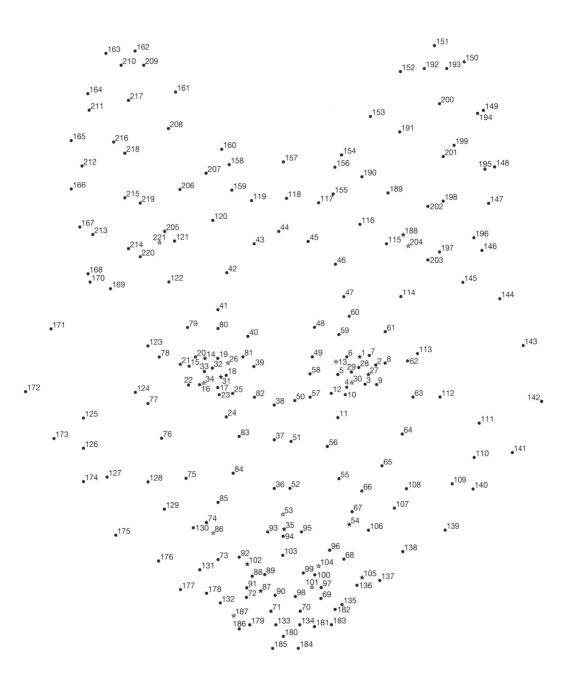

117: Fences

Solution on page 126

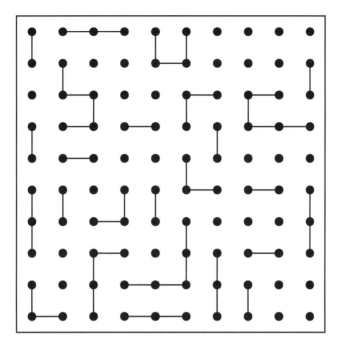

118: Fences

Solution on page 126

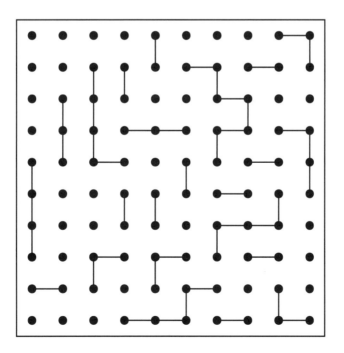

119: Spot the difference

Solution on
page 127

There are 20 differences to find.

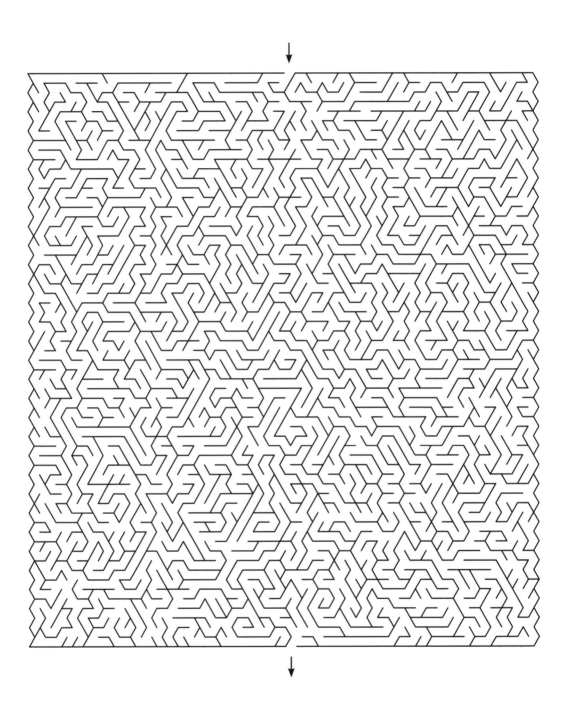

122: Sudoku

Solution on page 127

		6		5		3		
	3		4		6		2	
2			8		9			1
	9	8				5	3	
7								2
	2	1				4	8	
3			5		2			4
	7		9		3		5	
		2		7		9		

123: Sudoku

Solution on page 127

	6		9	3	8		5	
9								3
		7		4		9		
7			4	2	1			8
1		8	7		6	5		4
6			8	5	3			9
		1		7		4		
5								7
	7		3	1	4		9	

Solution on page 127

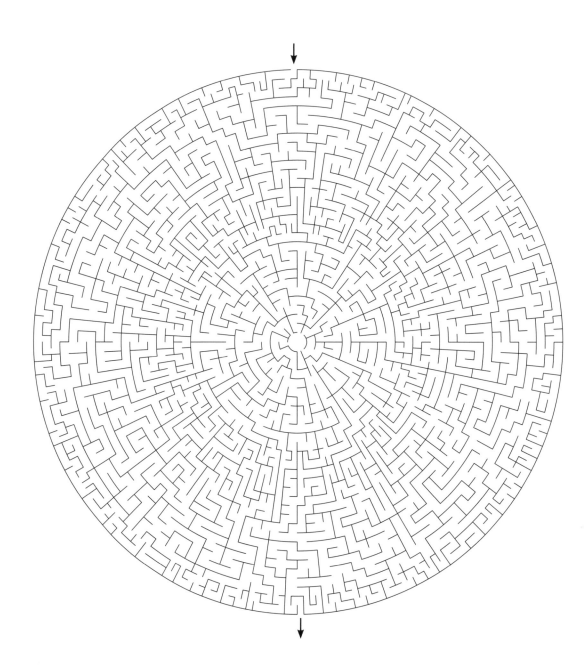

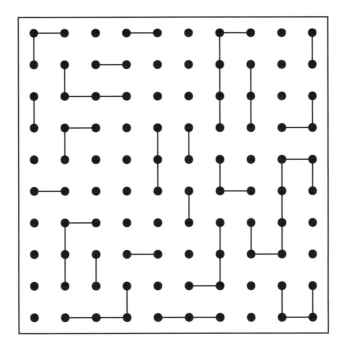

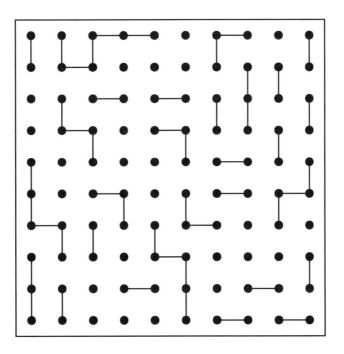

Across
1 Actual; real (5-2)
5 Vestibule (5)
9 Working well together (13)
10 Denote (8)
11 Enemies (4)
12 War shout (6,3)
16 Spouse (4)
17 Thick fabric with vertical ribs (8)
19 Business organizer (13)
21 Alter (5)
22 Turns the mind (7)

Down
2 Are plentiful (6)
3 Reproduce (9)
4 Last Greek letter (5)
6 Not at home (3)
7 Arcs (6)
8 Erase (6)
11 Lucky (9)
13 Ploy (6)
14 Haphazard (6)
15 Withdraw from a role (3,3)
18 Gave five stars, perhaps (5)
20 Small hotel (3)

128: On the river

Solution on
page 128

```
D E D C S A E S W A S A R S S
D N E B E O H S E S R O H T R
N I N H E O O S D O M M S Y E
E L S C A N A L R L C O E N D
S R N C W U H I T S P R T T N
T E B E S Y V N R G O I R V A
U T O S C E E R N S Y I L Y L
A A O L R M O I I L B H N Y S
R W O B I C R O R U A C E R I
Y C E D K O N E T Y H L B L T
K D E S O O Y A R A L O E A S
N S A M W R R H N A S L O E L
B A R G E Y C N V I D B L O A
N S N R C E E B S B A N K S D
D A M W O L F E C A F R U S C
```

BANKS
BARGE
BOAT
CANAL
CHANNEL
DAM
EROSION
ESTUARY
FLOW
HORSESHOE BEND
ISLAND
LOCK
MOORING POSTS
RIVERBED
ROCKS
SEDIMENT
SURFACE
TRIBUTARY
VALLEY
WATERLINE

129: Sudoku

Solution on page 128

7			1		2			4
		3				7		
	9			3			2	
6			7		3			9
		8				5		
4			5		9			1
	6			7			3	
		4				9		
3			2		4			8

130: Sudoku

Solution on page 128

		5				2		
			7	5	8			
1				2				4
	2		8		3		1	
	3	4				8	6	
	8		6		2		4	
3				8				5
			9	1	6			
		6				9		

131: Angular Maze

Solution on
page 128

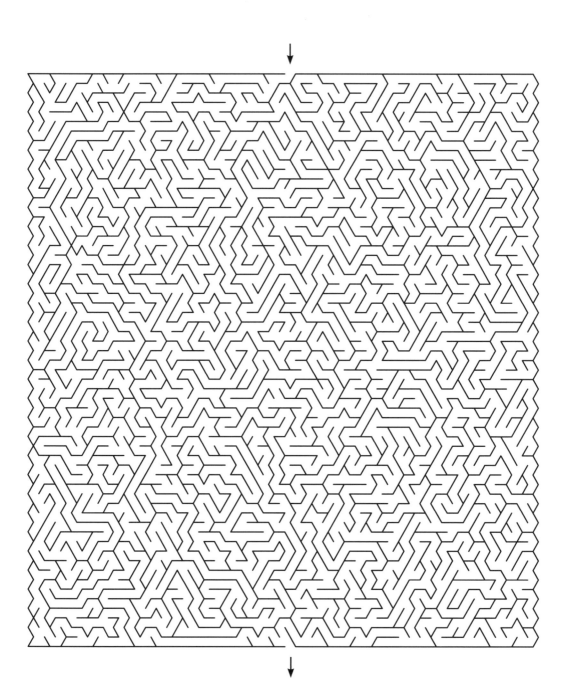

2

3

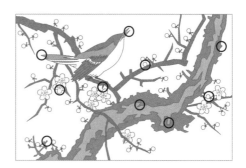

4

5

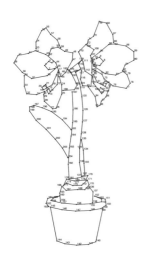

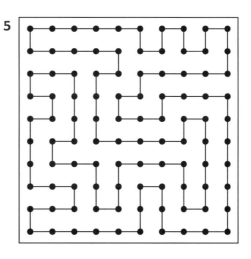

6

8

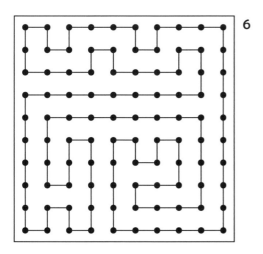

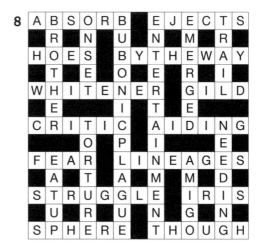

Solutions

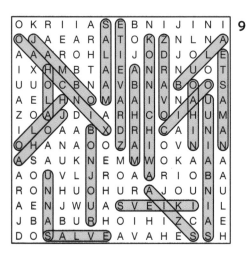

9

10

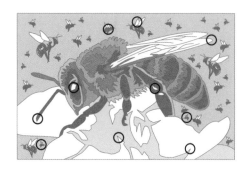

Wedding cake

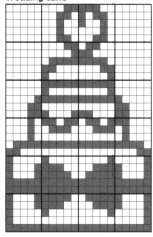

11

13

14

16

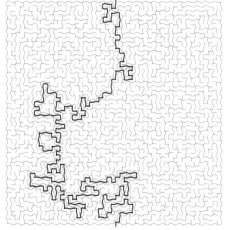

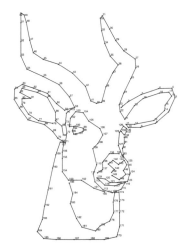

17

I		H		S				U		V		I
M	A	E	S	T	R	I		T	R	E	S	S
P		R		Y		N		M		L		P
L	O	B		M	Y	T	H	O	L	O	G	Y
I				I		R		S		C		
C	R	U	D	E		O	U	T	L	I	N	E
I		N		D		D			T		X	
T	A	B	L	E	A	U		L	A	Y	U	P
		I		D		C		I			O	
C	L	A	R	I	F	I	E	S		W	A	S
U		S		T		N		T		I		U
T	H	E	R	E		G	R	E	A	T	E	R
S		D		D				D		S		E

18

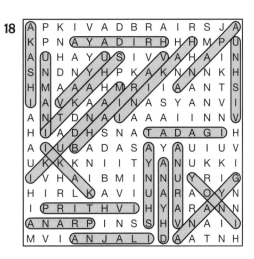

19

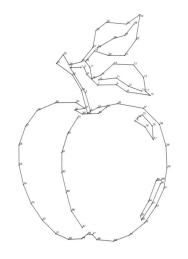

21

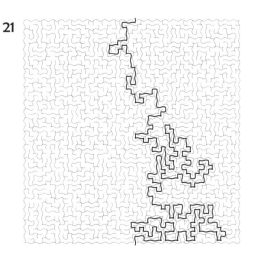

23

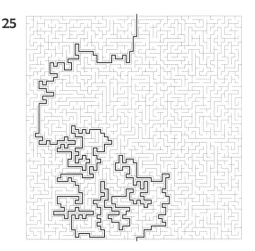

25

Solutions

27

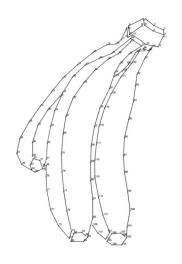

28

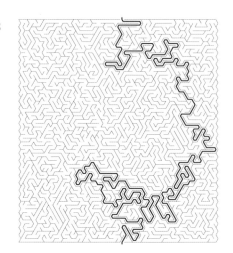

30

31

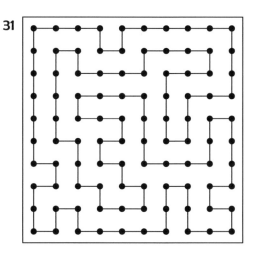

33

34

Solutions

Owl in front of the moon

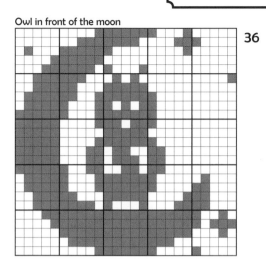

36

37

P	A	R	S	N	I	P		M	O	C	H	A
	B		U		N		M		I		A	
C	O	N	C	E	P	T	U	A	L	I	Z	E
	A		C		U		S		A			
O	R	I	E	N	T	A	L		D	I	R	E
	D		S				I		O		D	
		E	S	P	I	O	N	A	G	E		
	S		O		N			E			P	
H	A	I	R		R	E	V	E	A	L	E	D
	M				U		I		T		A	
C	O	R	R	E	S	P	O	N	D	I	N	G
	S		I		H		L		O		U	
R	A	B	B	I		N	A	U	G	H	T	Y

38

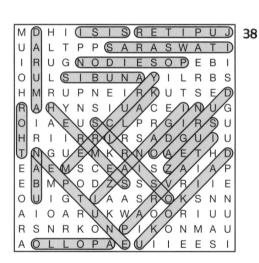

40

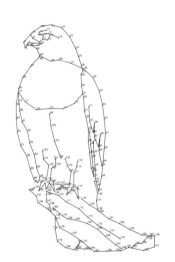

42

8	4	2	9	6	5	1	7	3
1	5	9	4	3	7	2	8	6
7	6	3	2	1	8	5	4	9
5	7	8	3	2	6	9	1	4
6	3	1	8	9	4	7	5	2
9	2	4	5	7	1	6	3	8
4	9	6	7	5	3	8	2	1
3	1	7	6	8	2	4	9	5
2	8	5	1	4	9	3	6	7

43

4	7	5	1	8	9	6	2	3
9	6	1	5	3	2	7	4	8
3	2	8	4	7	6	9	5	1
7	1	6	8	2	5	4	3	9
2	9	3	6	1	4	5	8	7
8	5	4	7	9	3	2	1	6
1	8	2	9	4	7	3	6	5
5	4	9	3	6	8	1	7	2
6	3	7	2	5	1	8	9	4

44

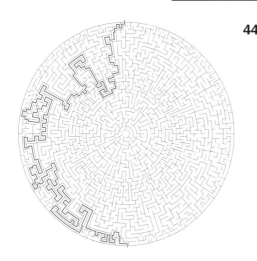

46

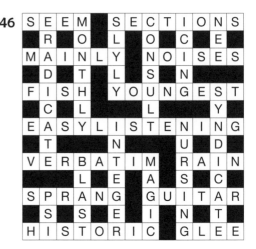

47

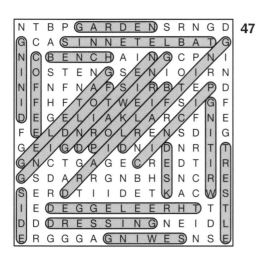

49

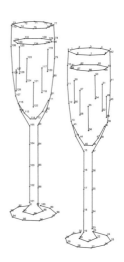

51

53

Solutions

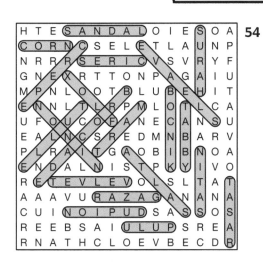

54

55

On top of a hill with a flag

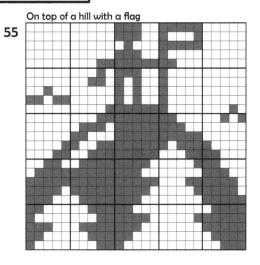

56   **57**

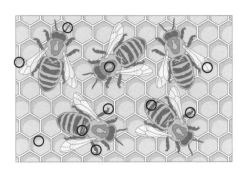

59   **60**

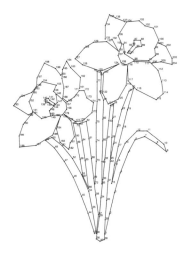

Solutions

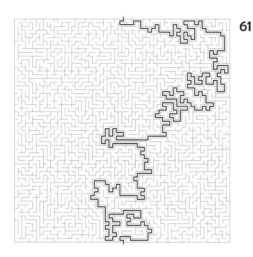

61

63

64

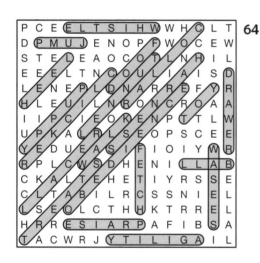

65

67

8	4	9	2	5	3	1	7	6
6	5	2	7	8	1	4	3	9
3	7	1	6	4	9	2	8	5
1	6	4	8	7	5	3	9	2
2	9	8	4	3	6	7	5	1
7	3	5	1	9	2	8	6	4
4	2	7	9	6	8	5	1	3
9	1	3	5	2	7	6	4	8
5	8	6	3	1	4	9	2	7

68

8	9	1	5	6	7	2	3	4
4	7	5	3	9	2	1	8	6
2	6	3	8	1	4	5	9	7
3	1	2	9	7	6	4	5	8
9	8	4	2	5	3	6	7	1
7	5	6	4	8	1	3	2	9
6	2	7	1	3	8	9	4	5
1	3	9	7	4	5	8	6	2
5	4	8	6	2	9	7	1	3

Solutions

69

71

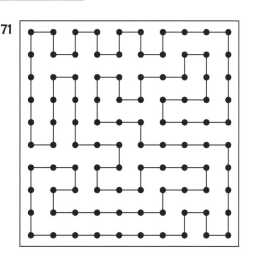

72

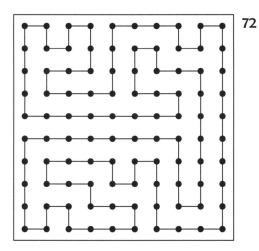

73

75

T	E	M	P	E	R	A	T	U	R	E	S	
R		A		W		V		P		O		A
A	G	R	E	E		A	R	S	E	N	I	C
N		M		R		T		T				C
S	N	A	G		M	A	H	A	R	A	N	I
M		L		P		R		I		P		D
I	N	A	W	A	Y		T	R	I	P	L	E
S		D		R		F		S		O		N
S	C	E	N	A	R	I	O		T	I	L	T
I			D		E			D		N		A
O	B	T	A	I	N	S		U	N	T	I	L
N		O		G		T		S		E		L
	F	R	O	M	D	A	Y	T	O	D	A	Y

76

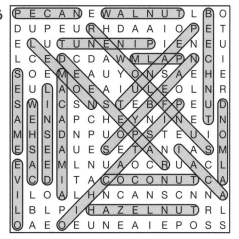

Solutions

Armchair

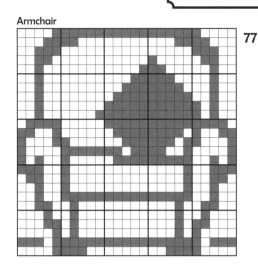

77

78

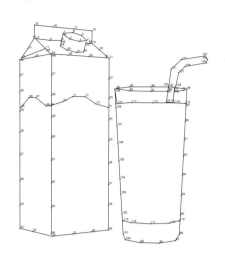

4	5	9	3	8	7	2	6	1
8	3	1	2	5	6	7	4	9
6	7	2	1	9	4	3	5	8
9	4	8	6	1	3	5	2	7
7	2	5	8	4	9	6	1	3
3	1	6	5	7	2	8	9	4
2	9	3	4	6	8	1	7	5
1	8	4	7	2	5	9	3	6
5	6	7	9	3	1	4	8	2

80

81

8	2	5	6	1	9	4	7	3
1	6	3	7	8	4	9	2	5
7	9	4	2	3	5	8	6	1
5	8	9	1	7	3	2	4	6
6	4	7	8	5	2	3	1	9
3	1	2	9	4	6	5	8	7
4	5	1	3	6	8	7	9	2
2	7	8	5	9	1	6	3	4
9	3	6	4	2	7	1	5	8

82

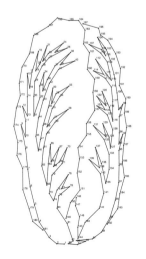

84

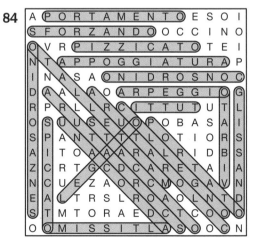

Solutions

85

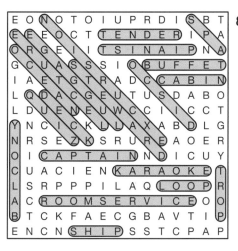

86

88

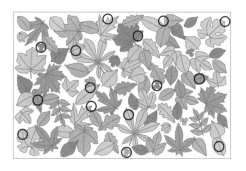

89

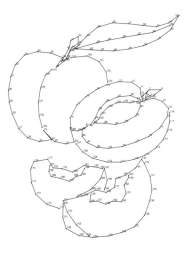

91

93

Solutions

94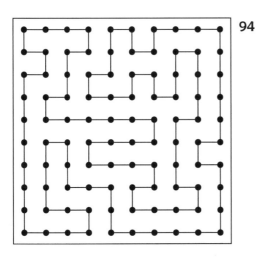

95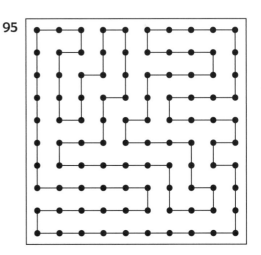

97

98

U	N	C	O	N	V	I	N	C	I	N	G	
N		H		O		N		O	U		B	
P	H	A	S	E		S	E	M	I	N	A	R
R		R		S		E		P			R	E
O	P	A	L		G	R	E	E	N	T	E	A
D		C		D		T		T		H		K
U	N	T	R	U	E		R	E	P	E	N	T
C		E		R		L		S		R		H
T	H	R	E	A	T	E	N		L	A	I	R
I			T		N		B		P			O
V	I	E	W	I	N	G		A	D	I	E	U
E		G		O		T		T		S		G
	D	O	W	N	T	H	E	H	A	T	C	H

99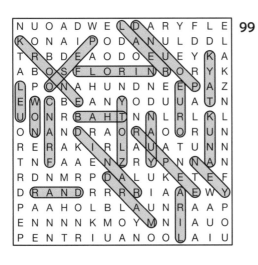

Calculator

101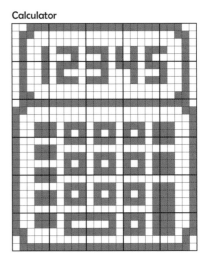

124

Solutions

102 **104**

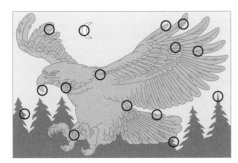

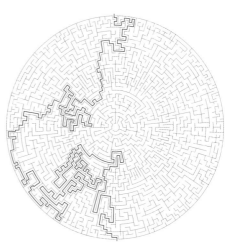

106 **108**

Pineapple

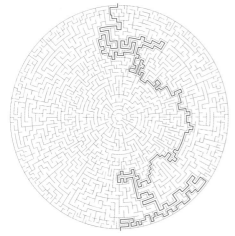

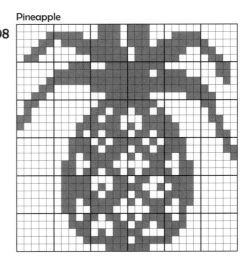

109 **110**

Solutions

111

| | M | I | S | A | N | T | H | R | O | P | Y | |
|S| |L| |D| |A| |U| |O| |C|
|H|E|L|T|E|R|S|K|E|L|T|E|R|
|E| |Q| |T| |D| |P| |A|
|L|E|C|T|U|R|E|S| |C|O|P|S|
|F| |O| |A| |D| |A| |U| |H|
| |F|O|N|T|S| |G|L|O|R|Y| |
|L| |P| |E| |R| |L| |R| |M|
|A|N|E|W| |D|E|F|I|N|I|T|E|
|U| |R| |A| |M| |N| |E| |A|
|G|U|A|R|D|I|A|N|A|N|G|E|L|
|H| |T| |D| |I| |L| |O| |S|
| |P|E|R|S|O|N|A|L|I|T|Y| |

112

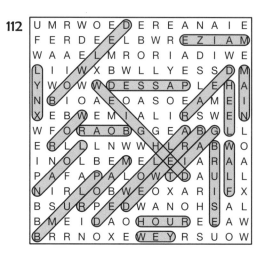

114

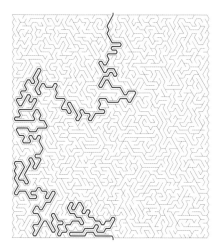

115

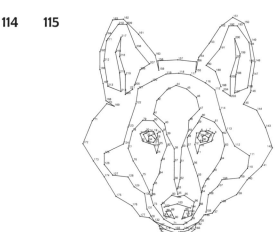

117

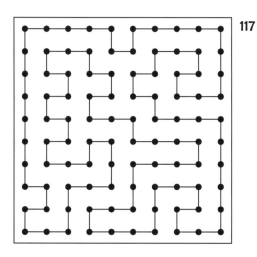

118

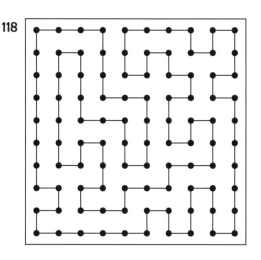

126

Solutions

119

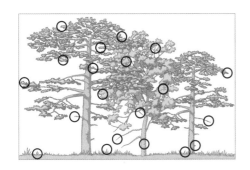

121

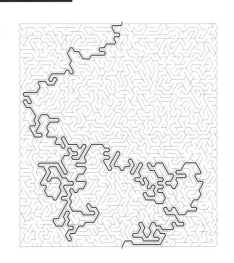

122

8	1	6	2	5	7	3	4	9
9	3	7	4	1	6	8	2	5
2	4	5	8	3	9	6	7	1
4	9	8	7	2	1	5	3	6
7	5	3	6	4	8	1	9	2
6	2	1	3	9	5	4	8	7
3	6	9	5	8	2	7	1	4
1	7	4	9	6	3	2	5	8
5	8	2	1	7	4	9	6	3

123

4	6	2	9	3	8	7	5	1
9	8	5	1	6	7	2	4	3
3	1	7	5	4	2	9	8	6
7	5	9	4	2	1	3	6	8
1	3	8	7	9	6	5	2	4
6	2	4	8	5	3	1	7	9
8	9	1	6	7	5	4	3	2
5	4	3	2	8	9	6	1	7
2	7	6	3	1	4	8	9	5

124

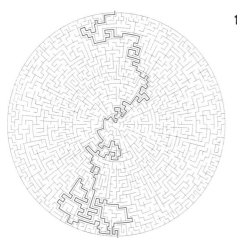

125

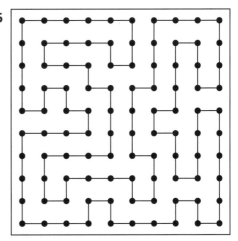

Solutions

126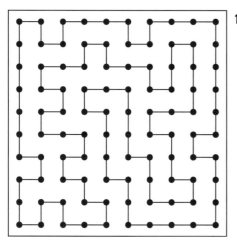

127

H	A	N	D	S	O	N	■	P	O	R	C	H
■	B	■	U	■	M	■	D	U	■	U	■	U
C	O	M	P	L	E	M	E	N	T	A	R	Y
■	U	■	L	■	G	■	L	■	V	■	■	■
I	N	D	I	C	A	T	E	■	F	O	E	S
D	■	C	■	■	■	T	■	O	■	S	■	■
■	B	A	T	T	L	E	C	R	Y	■	■	■
R	■	T	■	A	■	■	■	T	■	B	■	■
M	A	T	E	■	C	O	R	D	U	R	O	Y
■	N	■	■	T	■	A	■	N	■	W	■	■
A	D	M	I	N	I	S	T	R	A	T	O	R
■	O	■	N	■	C	■	E	■	T	■	U	■
A	M	E	N	D	■	A	D	V	E	R	T	S

128

```
D E D C S A E S W A S A R S S
O N E B E O H S E S R O H T R
N I N H E O O S D O M M S Y E
E L S C A N A L R L C O E N D
S R N C W U H I T S P R T T N
T E B E S Y V N R G O I R V A
U A O S C E E R N S Y I L Y L
A O L R M O I L B H N Y S
R W O B I C R O R U A C E R I
Y C E D K O N E T Y H L B L T
K D E S O O Y A R A L O E A S
N S A M W R R H N A S L O E L
B A R G E Y C N V I D B L O A
N S N R C E E B S B A N K S D
D A M W O L F E C A F R U S C
```

129

7	8	6	1	5	2	3	9	4
2	4	3	9	6	8	7	1	5
5	9	1	4	3	7	8	2	6
6	1	5	7	4	3	2	8	9
9	7	8	6	2	1	5	4	3
4	3	2	5	8	9	6	7	1
1	6	9	8	7	5	4	3	2
8	2	4	3	1	6	9	5	7
3	5	7	2	9	4	1	6	8

130

7	9	5	1	6	4	2	3	8
2	4	3	7	5	8	1	9	6
1	6	8	3	2	9	7	5	4
6	2	7	8	4	3	5	1	9
9	3	4	5	7	1	8	6	2
5	8	1	6	9	2	3	4	7
3	1	9	4	8	7	6	2	5
8	5	2	9	1	6	4	7	3
4	7	6	2	3	5	9	8	1

131